A kid begins to wonder how he/she will manage life, if the parents are unable.

A lot negative in our life starts from our childhood.

So, let's find out what to do with it...

Introduction

Do you wake up every morning and stop to think,
"How do I get through this day?" You simply get on with it.
Whether you realize it or not, your actions are direct results of
your thoughts.

You are what you think. You change from eating meat to
vegetables; go through the closet to pick the attire for the office,
business meeting or ball room dance at will. You go through life
the way a doctor does with a scalpel to get out ovarian cancer?
Self-development forms the foundation of success in life. What is
the secret to effective self-development?

Thinking for a change requires positive thinking, self-discipline
and self motivation in that order to realize true life transformation.
Positive thinking is the inward desire while action is the outward
demonstration of inner heart craving for self-development.

Your action confirm inner positive mental attitude. Actions lead to
expected self-development outcome in preferred area of interest
and choice. This book shows:

- You Create Your Thoughts.

- How Thoughts Shape Your Personality

- How Negative Thoughts Influence Outcome of Events.

- The Power of Positive Thinking.

- How to Setup Self-Development Foundation.

- How Self-Development Establish Success in Life.

- The Place of Positive Thinking Beyond Self-Development.

The first section of this book explores inward effect of self-development. This section covers chapter one to three. The second section of the book reveals outward demonstration of self-development.

Why write another book on self-development?
One of the challenges of most self-development programs is the emphasis on one aspect at the exclusion or neglect of the others. For example, psychology advances self-development from a psychological viewpoint. Religion links self-development to spirituality. Behavioral science looks at self-development from nature's point of view.

You learn how to blend three human aspects, the physical, the psychological and the spiritual to achieve effective self-development. Positive thinking discussed in this book is not a mental game of words.

So this is not just another book on self-development. This book takes a unique dynamic approach to self-development.

TABLE OF CONTENTS

How 3 Human Ignition Compartments Work

"The world we have created is a product of our way of thinking," Einstein said.

Did you know human beings have internal ignition compartments? But unlike the car, the three human ignition compartments take care of the physical, psychological and the spiritual aspects of life.

Digestive system is the first ignition compartment. Here the food is broken down and changed into energy. This energy gives the body strength to move around. Your body needs physical nourishment for up keep and maintenance.

Your brain is the assembly line for manufacturing negative and positive thoughts. If you like, the human brain is the informal sector, where ideas are turned into usable goods. The human brain is capable of formulating ideas from nothing. These ideas are processed into tangible items through body activity, the channel by which thoughts are put into action in the physical world.

Third, in every human beings heart there is avoid that can only be filled by supernatural being, many simply refer to as God. If any of these 3 internal ignition compartments is faulty the whole system is down. These three human ignition compartments work in harmony in self-development.

Chapter 1 - You Create Your Thoughts

Imagine living in a world in which all channels of communication are off air. How would you manage life without the internet, cable television network, local television, radio are off air and no daily newspaper in circulation? Life would be dead boring.

How about if you stopped thinking? You think all the time. But do you know the point at which thinking starts? When does thinking stop? Does death mark the end of thinking? These are hard questions. Chapter one shows connectivity of the body and brain, and suggests seven guidelines to assist you walk down the path of self-development with confidence.

Human Body and Brain Connectivity.

How does the body and brain work in harmony? The brain cannot function without a body. The body needs the brain to accomplish tasks. Your brain functions at peak when the body is at its best.

Think of body and brain connectivity in terms of car maintenance service. The body and brain need repair from time to time. How does the human body and brain servicing work? There are no spare parts for the body or brain. These two are renewed through the operating system in place.

1. Body Repair and Renewal Process.

Renewal of the body is a natural process. The body you showed up in on this planet has gone through a great deal of change. One or two strands of hair fly off every time you run a comb through the head. You might not notice.

You have a smooth patch on top of the head. You are truly bald. Only it didn't happen overnight. You have only noticed the change. But it has been happening all the time. But changes on the body continue all the time.

When you are dead asleep, the body and the brain systems go to work to repair and replace tired tissues. You are as good as new the next day. This human body and brain recycling therapy process is referred to as renewal.

2. Brain Revitalization Procedure.

Space exploration and invention of computers was the next big thing five decades ago. A decade ago, mobile phones hit the world market with a bang. In less than a decade, Smartphone has revolutionized individual lives around the globe like never before in human history.

Predictions of ten years to come might read as science fiction now but will shortly become old fashioned. Advanced technology is turning ordinary passive consumers into active producers. What is the source of this revolution? The human brain is the foundation of all ground breaking inventions.

Technology invention has limitations. You risk losing huge chunks of data stored in the computer, tablet or Smartphone. Human brain is the best information storage facility. It is easy to maintain. However, changing negative to positive thoughts is a daunting task. But, it is doable, if you set the mind to it.

"If you don't like something, change it; if you can't change it, change the way you think about it," Mary Eglebreit said. Chapter two details how thoughts shape your personality. We shall get to that in a bit. In the meantime, be encouraged and comforted that the human brain is the only broadcasting station that never goes off air. The question is where do thoughts come from?

Beliefs, childhood upbringing, and the environment influence the way you think. It is safe to say you create your own thoughts. Beyond that is mind boggling. Thoughts determine character. Character defines personality and personality shapes your self-image.

"Just as a gardener cultivates the plot, keeping it free from weeds…, so may a man tend the garden of his mind weeding out the wrong thoughts," James Allen wrote in the book "As A Man Thinketh."

Throughout this book, the emphasis on self-development focuses on positive thinking. Self-development is about making changes in your life. Real change starts in the brain. That is the unique approach this book adopts to achieve effective self-development through positive thinking.

Significance of Positive Thinking in Self-Development.

You have dreams. You have also acquired limiting attitudes which stand on the way as stumbling blocks preventing you from turning your dreams into reality. You talk to yourself about the things you wish to accomplish in life. But without changing your beliefs, the dreams remain buried under the rubble of negative thoughts as the brain battle rages on.

Brain Battle

Negative thoughts lead to frustration and failure. Positive thinking paves the way to success in life. You require a number of interventions to change negative to positive thinking. Imagine thinking,

"I can do this." Unfortunately, the words "I can't," come easy to most of us. Who says you can't? "I am not good enough," you think. Your internal conversation is dominated by negative thoughts. Is it any wonder you have not achieved any meaning effective self-development in life?

Your subconscious mind is conditioned to react negatively whenever you come up to a challenging task. You are offended if a family member or friend hints you don't have what it takes to accomplish a task. Yet you tell yourself "I can't," all the time without caring how negative thoughts influence the outcome. How can you navigate your way around negative thoughts? Think Positive. What is the significance of positive thinking in self-development?

1. Learn from A Child's Growth and Development

Children learn from parents in the early stages of growth and development. Most parents do not take time to examine the process of a child's growth. A child who grows up with criticisms has difficulty with poor self-image. But when the child is surrounded with love and clothed with the power of praise, he/she grows up with self-confidence. You can draw inspiration from such simple life experiences to accomplish tasks through positive thinking.

In another development, parents urge children to aim for the sun yet act different.

"We do not have money to buy you the $500 dollar video game. We cannot afford to pay rent on a three bedroom house," -parents lament.

A kid begins to wonder how he/she will manage life, if the parent's are unable. You are the kid's role model. Whatever you can or can't do, rubs off on kids.

Kids easily pick up negative signals from parents. Over period of time, negative mental attitude becomes part of a childhood upbringing. That is the downside. On the bright side of life, some kids grow in an environment surrounded with possibilities. Imagine how different the child would turn out if he/she grows up with words of encouragement, such as "you are the best kid on the block. You are smart, sensitive and sharp."
"Example is not the main thing in influencing others, it is the only thing," A proverb explains. It starts with your perspective to life.

If you improve others by being a good example, you also improve. People seldom improve when they have no example to follow other than themselves. You can be an example of shining light to the kids in one of two ways. Either you live as a candle, or a mirror that reflects it.

Chapter 1 – Summary

"The problem with most education institutions is that they try to teach people what to think, not how to think," John C. Maxwell wrote in the book "Thinking for A Change." Learning is not limited to education institutions. There no age restriction or shortage of new skills to learn including changing negative to positive thinking.

Chapter one shows the connectivity of human body and brain, and suggests seven guidelines to assist you walk down the path of self-development with confidence through positive thinking. Positive thoughts reaffirm your commitment to success. The more positive thoughts you have in mind, the greater the effect it has on self-development.

You know how thoughts are created. In chapter two, you will learn how thoughts shape your personality.

Chapter 2 - How Thoughts Shape Your Personality

Do you need to read another self-development book, blog post; listen to more motivational talk hoping negative thoughts will go away? Taking these steps could lift you out of frustration and failure. Great if that happens. However, it is not always the case.

Most people are overwhelmed by negative thoughts. It is not out of lack of books on self-development, not the number of blog posts and not the absence of motivational talks online, or from friends and family. What makes the difference?

The secret in dealing with negative thoughts is not reciting positive affirmations. You spend seven minutes to do that. What happens to the rest of the time? Your mind reverts to negative thoughts. Shifting of the mind to think positive has nothing to do with what type or how many positive affirmations you rehearse. It has everything to do with you. Until the two personalities, conscious and subconscious, work together in harmony, positive affirmations are no more than a band aid in self-development.

How many times, have you said, "I am self confident," yet felt afraid in the heart you could crawl into a hole? Your brain works with one item at a time to realize effective self-development in the area of preference. A lot more work and effort is required to realize change of attitude from negative to positive thinking. Let's face it. We all live through periods in life assailed by negative thoughts.

Positive thinking is the first step towards self-development. It is the vital link on the chain of other essential elements, which make self-development work. Effective self-development is based on improving physical, mental and spiritual aspect of life through positive thinking. How do you use positive thinking to your advantage? This chapter shows you seven different ways how to adjust and manage your thoughts to build a strong personality.

Seven Ways to Adjust and Manage Your Thoughts.

1. Acknowledge negative thoughts are real

Are you aware negative thoughts are holding you back from becoming the person your heart desires in life? "I have moved on from relationship breakup," you say, yet you are hurting, serves no purpose. Who are you fooling? Saying you are done having a temper while bottle resentment and bitterness inside is not good for your health. What good does it do you to say one thing and act different?

You are angry. That is natural. Telling a friend, I forgive you, as you stew with rage does not solve the situation. Self-evaluation does. Self-evaluation is the road map to self-development. Self-development without self-evaluation is similar to treating unknown disease. That is the reason doctors run tests on patients.

You can read books, subscribe to life coach blog posts listen to seasoned motivational speakers but unless you are ready for self-development, self development is not ready for you.

"When the student is ready, the teacher will show up," Zen proverb says. How do you evaluate yourself? Ask as many questions as come to mind to pin down why you are not living the life you deserve. Here are suggested questions to get you started.

What do I want out of life? This is the question on purpose for living.

How do I get what I want? This question is about the process.

Why is self-development important to my life? This question seeks to identify the outcome.

2. Hang out with Positive People

Tom, a friend, stops by from time to time for a chat to catch up on current affairs. The conversation runs on a cheerful note until the tone changes from items of mutual interest to personal problems.

Tom has his fair share of challenges. He is not shy to download his domestic and financial problems on me. So I sit and listen. But at the end of the conversation, I am exhausted. What do you tell such a friend?

You don't realize it, but negative people drain your energy fast. Yes, have friends, provided they don't drown you in the sea of negative thoughts. Negative thoughts rub off and influence not just the friend's personality but also yours, if left unchecked.

3. Examine Your Actions and Behaviors Frequently

You go through periods of swing moods. Your feelings, actions, and behaviors reflect your mood. In the school of life, you are the student, and coach all rolled up in one. You know when you are not in control of your life.

Check out your moods from time to time. Feelings are not carved on stone. If you are able to identify one or two negative feelings, you have a head start in gauging your mental health. Know when you are at your best to make adjustment and manage your thoughts without falling into pieces.

4. Your Views and Opinions Matter.

You have an opinion. Everyone is entitled to one. Your opinion of a situation is based on your perception and not anyone else's. You are unique, so is Joe Bloke or Jennifer Blanch.

The sky is blue is an accepted statement across the board by most people. But your blue is not 100% similar to someone else's. There is a slight variation in the sky's blueness. Having a different point of view has many advantages. For example, try using the left hand if you are right handed. It might feel awkward at first. A left handed person would feel the awkwardness as well. In reality, it is only a different point of view.

Self-discovery unlocks alternative methods of dealing with challenging issue in life including self-development to bring the best out of you.

5. Master Your Mind

Have you ever tried to get rid of all thoughts from your mind? You can if you want to. You have the power to block out all negative thoughts, and clear the mind. It is not easy, but it is doable. You might not succeed the first time but you will over period of time through trial and error.

My life had no sense of direction or purpose a decade ago. If I knew then what I know today, about positive thinking having read 35+ self-development books, my life would have turned out different. Positive thinking works.

If you clear the mind of all thoughts, you are capable of allowing only positive thoughts to occupy your brain data bank. Try it out. You discover the secret of power your mind wields over thoughts. This means, you choose to allow only positive thoughts to dominate the mind.

Imagine your mind as a clean slate. You are the only one with the pen that writes on it. Why not practice writing positive thoughts on it. Dr. Maxwell Maltz used CRAFT acronym in his ground breaking book "Psycho-Cybernetics," to show how to deal with thoughts. The five letters of this acronym represents a different word. C stands for Cancel, R - Replace, A - Affirmation, F – Focus, and Train

Dr. Maltz was a plastic surgeon. He also pioneered self-development to give his patients hope. Your situation might be different. But the principle is the same. In the absence of a better alternative way of dealing with thoughts, let's borrow Dr. Maltz CRAFT acronym. You might want to come up with your own way to unlock doors of opportunity through self-development to master your mind.

6. Imagination Unlocks Doors of Opportunity for Self-Development.

How different would life be without imagination? There would be no fiction books. Inventions would be hard to come by. These are only two items of value coming from imagination, and the list is only limited by your imagination. Imagination can be good or bad depending on the outcome of the event or activity. In chapter six, you will read more on the advantages and disadvantages of imagination.

Your brain has the power to create mental pictures of nonexistent situations through imagination. You visualize the outcome of events and tasks without sweat. You can use imagination in self-development to improve different areas of your life. This book shares seven areas of life open to self-development.

7. Stay focused to Rise Above Inward Struggle.

You are struggling to break free from the past. Every time a light shines on the path for self-development, a strong wind from the adversary blows over it violently, it's reduced to a flicker. How do you stay focused on self-development to achieve the ultimate price?

Keep your eyes fixed on the price. Listen to what your inner voice says. The third step on renewing the mind in chapter three explains the importance of listening to the inner voice in self-development. In the process, look out for available opportunities in life to live the life you envision.

If you are consumed about titles before and after your name, self-development would not satisfy your heart. Learn to define who you are. That is the only way to stay focused and rise above inward struggle.

Chapter 2 – Summary

How does the human brain work? The closest you can get to understanding how the brain works is to tune into the frequency of thoughts. Chapter two takes you through a short journey into the world of thoughts. You discover the power of thoughts by acknowledging thoughts are real.

Examine your actions and behaviors as you hang out with positive friends. Pay attention to different views and opinions including yours to master your mind with Dr. Maxwell Maltz acronym CRAFT. You will be amazed how imagination unlocks self-development doors of opportunity, if you stay focused and rise above inward struggle.

Chapter 3 - How Negative Thoughts Influence Outcome of Events.

Mental health presents most people with the biggest challenge. The reason is simple. Negative thoughts cannot be diagnosed in a laboratory or treated in health facility the way doctors treat diseases. That is only part of the challenge negative thoughts present in life.

The other challenge is how to get suitable cure for negative thoughts. These two together with other related issues lead many to seek different methods to overcome negative thoughts including but not limited to drowning sorrows in depression, looking at the problem from the bottom of liquor bottles.
It does not matter how much you drink to drown your sorrows or how hard you try to push negative thoughts out of the mind. Drinking might lull negative thoughts for a while, but as soon as you sober up, negative thoughts are back in full swing.

You cannot run or hide from negative thoughts. Negative thoughts go with you everywhere into Church, Mosque, and Synagogue, places revered for pure thoughts. Negative thoughts are similar in many ways to the monster Frankenstein created if you allow them to go out of control.

Chapter two shows you create your thoughts. Why can't you destroy negative thoughts before they destroy you? This chapter outlines four steps to overcome negative thoughts, and shows you three ways to transform your wife with positive thinking. Are you ready for the challenge? Let's do it with the four steps to overcome negative thoughts.

Four Steps to Overcome Negative Thoughts.

Step One - Identify the Negative Thought.

Negative thoughts are unnecessary inconveniences which disrupt normal body and brain functions. Negative thoughts cause anxiety, fear, stress and hopelessness. However, negative thoughts only become effective if you allow them to drive you nuts. Thoughts are emotions let loose to run wild in the brain.

If you can identify negative thoughts occurrence pattern, you have a foot inside the door of your brain to achieve a clean bill of mental health. You are capable of isolating negative thoughts. This is what the phrase, "You are what you think," is all about.

For example, there is no bad or good, only different weather. The weather condition is based on your interpretation. Negative thoughts are not harmful or bad, you make them. Your first baby step to rise above negative thought is to identifying the negative thought. You do that by discovering the pattern of your thoughts to distinguish negative from positive thoughts. This is not hard, provided you are up to the challenge. Here are three ways to get around this process.

1.   Pattern of Negative Thoughts.

You fret over bad business, lousy marriage, unstable income, failing health and fitness. Is worrying going to change things around? No. Action does. What do you expect thinking of the worst outcome? On the other hand,

"I am somebody. I can do this," pattern of thought makes a difference on the outcome. Your thoughts are yours alone but they are not you. Saying,

"I am ugly," does not make you ugly.

2. "Name and Shame," the Negative Thought.

You set unrealistic goals. You are held hostage by negative thoughts, if you set unrealistic goals. Dr. Daniel Siegel, author and psychiatrist came up with "name and tame," phrase to deal with negative thoughts. Call anxiety by its name, and shame it.

"I know you anxiety." Anxiety will not sneak up on you. You can smell it a mile away.

3. Live in the Moment.

"Life is a stage," William Shakespeare wrote. It is also a series of challenges. That is what makes life exciting. There is nothing wrong with thinking about the situation at hand. You are anxious over increasing declining age related health. You are as old as you believe and young as your heart desires.

It is true that the past forms the foundation of your life today. Without the past, the present and the future would be unheard of. Learn valuable lessons from the past to improve your present lifestyle as you anticipate a bright future through positive thinking. Dwelling in the past is counterproductive. You can't go back and undo what is done.

Your outlook on life defines your thoughts. Thoughts determine the kind of life you live now, not in the past, not in the future but in the moment. It is that simple and straightforward.

Step Two – Discover Sense of Direction

When you're young, naïve with no definite purpose, life is one enormous mysterious adventure. You grow up, mature and your focus in life sharpens. You think issues through before jumping onto the bandwagon of social mirror, peer pressure characteristic of the youth. You view things not so much out of the excitement and exuberance of youth but selectively with the wisdom that only old age accords.

In essence you're warming up to live life to the full. In William James words,
"I am just getting ready to live." I hope this is true of your life as it's mine. Step aside. Let the mind wander away. It will come back to you again.

You are mourning the death of a loved one. Thinking of the worst
will not bring the person back to life. Get a grip on reality.
Discover your voice in the middle of tragedy. That is the sense of
direction you need to move on. This is the second logical step you
take to triumph over negative thoughts. "I need to clear my head,"
is a hint to renew the mind and chart a new sense of direction.

Step Three – Renew the Mind Frequently

Transformation begins with inner awakening. You don't need anything from outside to set inner awakening in motion. There is no price tag hang on this invaluable unlimited commodity your life depends on. Your guiding compass, the inner voice is in place. Inner voice is first mentioned in chapter two to assist you stay focused. Chapter five further explains the function of the inner voice.

There are no restrictions, no requirements and no references needed from anyone to renew the mind. The resource for inner awakening is available and accessible anytime. Draw from the well that never runs dry – the brain. Inner awakening is your ticket to satisfaction, peace of mind and heart, plus a great deal more.

Step Four – Battle of the Brain

Nothing comes easy and cheap in life. You want to defeat negative thoughts in self-development, be prepared for the battle of the brain. This is the fourth step in dealing with negative thoughts. In this final step, ask and answer the following questions.

1. **What is the significance of this nagging negative thought in my head?**

This question establishes the outcome. You need to know whether the nagging negative thought adds or takes away what you already know about the outcome of the situation.

2. **Is there evidence showing what I am thinking of has grounds?**

Get supporting evidence from facts.

3. How helpful or harmful is this negative thought?

This third question foreshadows outcome. Visualize the destination or outcome of the event in the change process.

These three questions in the fourth step reflect on dealing with negative thoughts set the stage for your life transformation, starting with discovering purpose, process of change to achieving the price. Think of the four steps in this first section of chapter three as the bridge between where you are now and where you want to be with self-development. The next section of chapter three provides action plan to real life transformation process.

Real Life Transformation Process.

A friend or family member has disappointed you. Your work is no longer exciting. The relationship that once delighted you is lousy. There is always something to gripe about in life. That makes life hard to predict, but interesting to live. Can you walk away from life's disappointing experiences? Yes, you can with three simple methods.

1. Observe the Signs and Symptoms.

What is the first thing doctors look for in diagnosing a disease? If you are running a fever and the temperature is shooting up, you have a headache. Sending you to provide stool specimen for laboratory test is limited by the symptoms. The treatment for headache or any disease is arrived at through observing signs and symptoms. Let's leave diagnosis to the experts in that field.

There is no prescription drug for self-development. Low salary grievance is up to you. If the salary and remuneration board is not ready to revise salary scale, take up a course; learn a new skill with better pay package. Set yourself up for a raise. Stay on the job or quit. You have ample options.

You have difficulty with overweight body. Get advice on dieting and exercise from experts but the action to lose weight is yours. If a friend is taking advantage of your hospitality, show him/her the door. You can't forever hold his/her hand. Do yourself and the friend a favor, lean on him/her a little.

You can learn a new skill to improve your chances of salary raise, lose weight, start and run business to gain financial stability if you observe the signs and symptoms to discover suitable solution.

2. Switch Camps.

The moment you let the words, "I can't," roll out of your mouth, you dismiss any possibility of giving success a second chance. What are the odds when you say "I can't?" Saying I can't quit smoking is similar to committing suicide. You know the dangers of cigarette smoking on your lungs. You are aware defective lungs signal the end of life.

Think about it. You didn't start smoking by pronouncing the words, "I can't smoke cigarettes." Why should these words determine whether you should quit smoking or not? What is so hard about changing the way you communicate within? Is it harder to say "I can," than I can't?"

Changing from negative to mental attitude is a daunting task. It is difficult, no doubt, but, it is possible. Think of the successes you have had in the past. What made the difference? Your mental attitude towards self-development did. Good or bad habits are not set on stone. You can change them if you want by taking control of your life to switch camps.

3. Take Control of Your Life.

You are willing to change. Look within you for strength. A suitable solution is not out there somewhere. It's within provided you are ready to take responsibility for your actions in one of two ways.

  ✓ Be brutally honest with yourself.

Don't be deceived. Get facts about your financial status, marriage, career, leisure, health and fitness straight. Chapter two and five suggest you listen to the inner voice. You can't go wrong with the direction the inner voice gives. Be honest with yourself.

✓ Be willing to give in order to get something.

A friend is draining your energy with negative talk. Be willing to leave the friend out of the circle of your friends. Making the sacrifice to let go creates room to take a fresh look at the situation in life. It it's a habit such as smoking, drop it before it drops you six feet under.

The doctor might recommend cutting you up for a good reason. You lose something to gain your health back. If you let people walk all over you or take advantage of your kindness, you turn control of your life over to them.
Chapter 3 – Summary

Majority of construction workers on site are paid less than the architect standing over the drawing board in a posh office overlooking the beach. The architect is paid to think and come up innovative building blue prints, while construction workers sweat it out on site to earn a living. Would you rather sweat out or think in life?

This chapter suggests you take four steps to rise above negative thoughts. The four steps require you to identify nagging negative thoughts, discover a new sense of direction in life, renew your mind, to win the brain battle. Taking these four steps sets you up for real life transformation if you observe signs and symptoms of negative thoughts to take control and change your life.

Chapter 4 - The Power of Positive Thinking in Self-Development

You are willing to do whatever it takes to learn a new skill. That is because your heart is on fire to improve one or all areas of life. Nothing or no one can stop you.

None of the early inventors had available information to make breakthrough as you do online today. But they had positive mental attitude. The power of positive thinking set them apart from the rest of the crowd. These fine individuals conceived ideas through positive thinking and did not concede defeat until the ideas sprouted wings and flew.
This was the case with F.B. Morse's telegraph project, Thomas Edison's electric bulb. We could go on name dropping and come with a long list of who is who in history that came up with items of value to humanity. Not everyone is privileged to invent the wheel. It is not out of lack of inspiration or positive thinking, the two requirements for change. We shall never know about those who tried and failed.

In this chapter on the power of positive thinking, you will learn Eight Ways to Rekindle the Brain by Improving the Body, and Six Must Do Things to Stimulate Positive Thinking.

You are wondering why you need to improve the body first to rekindle the brain. In chronological order of creation, the body is formed first, and the heartbeat, your life containing organ comes next six to seven weeks after conception. This is proven scientific discovery.   Let's set the ball rolling with Eight Ways to Rekindle the Brain by Improving the Body.

Eight Ways to Renew the Brain by Improving the Body.

Your body flourishes on eating healthy foods, drinking plenty of water, having regular exercise, getting enough sleep, hanging out with friends and managing stress to live on purpose. The underlying principle behind these activities is to make the brain function at peak; prevent brain deterioration, which lead to anxiety, depression due to excessive brain exhaustion. You are not only what you think. You are also what you eat.

1. Meal Prepping

Does the phrase "meal prepping," ring a bell? Why should it not. You live in a world preoccupied with healthy eating, in which the term "meal prepping," has crept into everyday language.
Your brain, the decision making organ in the body uses 20% of energy from the food you eat to keep the body healthy, yet the brain is only 2% of the body weight, according to scientific research study outcome. These research studies prove the body needs special care and attention to enhance brain performance.

2. Drink Plenty of Water

Did you know the human body is made up of 75% water? Human body uses up water fast. You need to replenish water supply to the body or risk dehydration. Dehydration causes dizziness, idleness, indecision among other signs.

Water is good for the overall body and mental health. In addition, water, gets rid of harmful toxic waste in the body system. Thirst is the body alert system; ignore it at your peril. Drinking plenty of water prevents dehydration. You cannot over drink water.

3. Regular Exercise

Health is everyone's right and privilege.   You are sluggishness points to lack of exercise. You cannot exercise on an empty stomach. The body needs well balanced diet, in order to engage in meaningful regular exercises.

Your body functions best with regular exercises. 40 minutes, three times a week is all the time the body needs to stay healthy and fit. Exercise boosts the body immune system to fight diseases. Regular exercise injects fresh blood and air into the brain to make it perform at peak.
Take care of your body now, and it will take care of you in the years to come. Improve age related failing health with regular exercise.

4. Get Enough Sleep

Sleep does a lot more to the body and brain than all the other activities of the body put together. You are fresh in the morning having gone to bed dog tired the previous night. While you are dead asleep, the body system goes to work to repair and replace tired old body tissues. Lack of sleep could cause diabetes, heart disease and dementia.

Power nap is a great way to re-energize the body. You have a little time in the day to nap, go for it.

5. Managing Stress

Running broadcasting stations 24/7 is a great deal of work. Viewers and listeners of television and radio programs do not want to know how you get news, plan for talk shows or what you do to produce recorded programs and fillers.

This lot is spoilt for choice. You risk losing them to rival broadcasting stations. That means loss of revenue from advertisers which translate to the stations life cycle. Effective management plays a huge role in keeping the radio station on air.

This is the same principle behind body and brain renewal chapter one talks about. You risk dementia and other age related ailments by allowing stress to take over. What can you do to keep the mind attentive and alive? Meditation, getting enough sleep, hanging out with friends, listening to music, and reading are some of the activities responsible for rekindling the brain.

"Reading activates and exercises the mind," Dr. Ben Carson points out in his book, "Think Big, Unleashing Your Potential for Excellence." In addition,

"Reading forces the mind to discriminate," Dr. Carson adds and concludes with,
"Reading pushes us to use our imagination and makes us more creatively inclined."

.

6. Meditation is the Best Relaxation

Meditation is mostly associated with spiritual practice to gain higher self status. Meditation is good for mental health. Whether you are a spiritual person or not, having control over your thoughts, is the first step towards effective self-development.

Individual internal communication is not a new practice. Your decision making ability is linked to self talk. Self talk can be negative or positive. You have no way of knowing what the other person thinks. But you are aware of what you are thinking of all the time. Thoughts good or bad are exclusive to the individual.
You have developed different techniques to face life's challenges over the years. You want a clear picture of your life 5, 7, 10 years to come. Visualize it in the theatre of your imagination. If you want positive thoughts engraved in the mind, deliberate over them frequently. That is what meditation does.

7. Hang out with Friends.

You need a life outside of work, business. You learn a lot of new ideas from social interactions with friends. Let's not get carried away here and confuse social life and social media. Social life and media share a common denominator - friends. Time and space would not allow us to compare and contrast similarity and difference between these two.

All said and done, social media has advantages and disadvantages. We shall steer clear to walk down that road for now. You get to read more on friends in the next section on six must do things to stimulate positive thinking.

8. Get More Living out of Life.

Your interpretation of situations in life influences the outcome of events. You are passionate about something. How well do you know yourself? What makes you stand out in the crowd?

You share a lot in common with others but not your thoughts. Your thoughts are yours alone. You are original masterpiece. You are different and special. You are also unique. That means no one can fulfill your purpose in this life.

Why am I here?" This is one of four fundamental life questions; you need to ask in order to get more life out of living.

Six Must Do Things to Stimulate Positive Thinking.

1. Put the Past Down in Writing.

Have you ever sat down with a pen and paper to write down your failures in life? You do it with accomplishments, not failures. Writing clarifies things in the mind. One, you acknowledge short comings. Two, you get the opportunity to study the situation and possibly discover away to handle it next time. Three, put them behind. Sounds great, so let's put this idea into perspective.

You come up to a challenging situation and the two words that come to mind are "I can't." Remember to use Dr. Maxwell Maltz CRAFT acronym in dealing with negative thoughts from chapter two.

Cancel and replace "I can't," with "I can." Take one step ahead to affirm your desire with action as you focus the mind on the outcome. Your brain is wired to throw up positive outcome of the situation or event at hand through these five simple steps Dr. Maltz used to give hope to his plastic surgery patients

2. Put Your Life into Perspective.

No one convenes a press conference, or sends out press releases detailing his/her failures. It is always something good about to happen. If positive thinking is the in thing, how come success stories are fewer than failures in life? That is the bad news.

But here is the good news. You can improve on things you failed to achieve in the past. 'Why bother if the past is unchangeable?" You ask. Sure you cannot change the past. What is done is done. But you can change the way you think now to improve your present lifestyle and future prospects.

3. Stop the Blame Game

You blame other people, situations, over failures but not you. Spouses blame one another when the marriage breaks down. The husband or wife caused it. It is easy to notice fault with someone else, hard to take a long hard look at self. F.B. Morse could have blamed the government for withholding funds to put his telegraph project into practice. He did not. He trained the mind to stay positive.

In one of his letters, Morse wrote,

"…knowing from long experience whence my help must come in hours of difficulty, I soon disposed of all my cares, dropped to sleep, and rested the remainder of the night as quietly as a little child." That is beautiful. Keep trying like a child.

A child keeps on training his/her muscles until he/she learns to walk alone. You too can train and strengthen your mind muscles to think positive.

4. Strengthen the Mind

Your mind can stand against anything the body can't handle. The body depends on the mind for guidance and direction. Athletes don't wake up on the day of the big game, dressed up to win.

They train for hours over periods of time to make the team selection for the upcoming events. During training, the body is put to the test. But winning is in the mind. Whether you are thinking of starting a business, losing weight, developing career, starting a family, falling in love, it's all in the mind. You cannot exhaust the brain power potential. Your achievements in life are only limited by your imagination.

5. Time Together with Friends

You need friends for encouragement, bounce off ideas, and for companionship. Not all friends fulfill these needs. Remember my friend Tom mentioned in chapter two is a burden rather than a blessing kind of friend. Yes, by all accounts make friends and enjoy the time of your life together with friends. But choose your friends wisely.

Associate with friends sharing common values in life. You might as well read biographies of people that inspire you than spend time with a friend like Tom.

6. Is No News Good News?

Pick up the morning paper, watch late night television or listen to radio news; you think there is nothing good happening in life. Media thrives on bad news. But all life is not gloom? Of course, there are moments of sadness in life.   There are also periods of happiness and excitement.

The tendency is to dwell on the dark side of life. How can you move on to prosperity, if your mind is locked on negative thoughts? You miss the opportunity of discovering the good present in the seemingly bad situations in life.

You are aware of tons of examples. Think of those living with physical challenges. Many of these individuals manage life without grumbling. How do they do it? Chapter six makes reference to my own life experience to illustrate the power of positive thinking. Be sure to read it.

Ask any person living with disability and the answer is simple. "I changed my way of thinking and my life changed." You can read, watch videos, and listen to brilliant ideas from experts. But until thought is linked to idea through common sense, the idea will not develop wings and fly on its own.

Chapter 4 – Summary

Human beings are fitted with Operating System to take care of eventualities in case of emergency. Individual personal values, career development, finances, relationship, marriage, family, health and fitness are the main areas of self-development.

This chapter explains how to renew the mind by improving the body through meal prepping, drinking plenty of water, regular exercise, sleeping well, managing stress, meditation, to get more living out of life.

Engage in six must do things to stimulate positive which include, writing down failures, putting life into perspective, strengthening the mind, and hanging out with friends. How do you know self-development is right for you now? Discover whether self-development is right for you in chapter five, next.

Chapter 5 - How to Setup Self-Development Foundation

Scientific discovery point out most people use 5% of the brain power. The 5% active brain power is also invaded by negative thoughts. 95% valuable human brain power potential is not exploited. This explains why you think,

"I am not good enough." What standard of measurement do you use to arrive at this conclusion? You are the best there is, and will be. How do you overcome fear? Dale Carnegie has the right piece of advice,

"If you want to conquer fear, don't sit home and think about it. Go out and get busy." Try it out and be the judge. Fear sucks up most of your body energy. Think about it. What good does fear bring into your life?

Whether, you are falling in love, taking time off work to spend quality time with the family, making a career change decision or gearing up for self-development. You know when something is right.

This chapter shows you how positive mental attitude sets the foundation for self-Development. When the foundation is in place, use three human being aspects, the physical, psychological and spiritual to build on self-development foundation.

Three Simple Actions Set Up Self-Development Foundation.

You don't turn a friend away by telling him/her to get a grip on reality just because he/she is feeling low. You are more considerate and sympathetic to others than you are to self. You don't believe it? Sofia Rydin-Gray director of health psychology at Duke Diet Fitness Centre Durham NC does. Here is what Sofia says,

"If a friend came to you feeling down, would you beat them over the head? Probably not… But we often do that to ourselves." How do you setup self-development foundation through positive mental attitude?

1.   Be Nice not Nasty to Self.

You might have set unrealistic high standards in one or more areas. You come down hard on self,

"I am not good enough." You have made the conclusion without evaluating the situation in order to discover the cause of failure. Negative thinking is reinforced in the brain data bank through negative thoughts put into words. The ripple effect spreads to other areas of your life as well. Retrace your thoughts. Go back to the drawing board. Ask what you did wrong or didn't do right. You will discover the missed step in the process.

People used maps to find their way around new locations in the old days. Today, you have apps to take you from A-Z. Grace, our second born daughter sent me WhatsApp detailing how she uses app to locate places in America when she is on vacation while her husband is finalizing the process of defending his doctoral dissertation thesis. Cute huh! But it is up to the individual to get to the destination. The app is accurate. However, if you don't follow the instructions you wind up in a different location.

You want to lose weight. Invest in a good diet book, or join a gym. Next time you step on the scale in three weeks, you have put on an extra kilogram.

"This is not working," you think. This statement sends a negative message to the subconscious mind from the conscious. The book promised you would lose weight in three weeks. However, two things might have happened. One, your body is wired differently. Two, you might have missed a step in the process. None of these two reasons warrant dismissing the program as not working. Saying,

"This is not working," sets you up for failure instead of success. You are concerned about health and fitness; reengineer your mind with positive thinking. Tell yourself,

"It didn't work out in three weeks but I am not giving up." Challenge the mind as much as you challenge the body. Refuse to give up. You will not lose weight if you quit. Keep on going. You didn't pack all the extra kilos in the body at once. You will not shed it all off in a flash. Positive mental attitude set you up for self-development in the field of preference.

2. Hang on to Progress – Life Depends on It.

You are using a map for direction. You have been walking for hours. You realize you have missed the destination. Hang on to the progress you have made. Take a peek at the app again to get back on track. You don't want to go back all the way home to start all over again. It is time and energy consuming. You made some progress. Hang on to the progress as you correct course to get to the preferred destination.

Another example is in recovery from sickness. You have been in hospital for a month. During this time, the body is not active. The muscles are weak due to lack of exercise. However, the doctor's regular rounds show steady health progress and you are discharged.

Re-entering the world of activity you left behind presents a big challenge to gain composure. The doctors have done their part. It is your turn to exercise and get the body back in shape. Start small and increase regular exercise gradually to get back to normal life activity. Let positive mental attitude guide and give you direction on the road to recovery. Hang on to positive thoughts and the progress on the road to recovery.

3. If You are Fired Up - Failure is not an Option.

Let us use the example of losing weight above for illustration. How much do you want to lose weight? If failure is not an option, you will not settle for less than the best. Your reaction to putting on the extra kilo of weight sets the next step.

"This is not working," is a negative reaction. Positive thinking prompts self-evaluation questions.

"Did I exercise for forty minutes, thrice a week? What foods have I eaten these past three weeks?" Questioning your behavior and actions provide feedback to assist you discover what you did or did not do right. Professor S. Dweck, PhD Psychologist at Stanford University observed that your success mindset leads to developing good or bad habits.

Five Non-Negotiable Principles Reveal Self-Development is Right for You.

1.   Trust Your Instincts.

"We are right for each other," one couple shared in a magazine interview featuring newlyweds. No reasoning can change how you feel about someone or something of value. The only way to confirm your heart is in the right place is to go through self-development process.

Call it gut feeling, sixth sense or prompting of the inner voice, it boils down to instinct. This is not a departure from reasoning. Reason to make sure self-development is right for you now. Trust your instincts.

2. Take the Next Big Step Now.

Success in life is only limited by individual action to allow the idea blossom. You have nursed the idea of changing careers. You know the time is right. Any further delay might result in missed opportunity to get to the next level. Take the next step now. Sandra was intrigued by selling beauty care products to local saloons in the community.

She got in touch with a supplier and struck a deal. This move set her plans in motion. In six months the business had picked up and paid off. Sandra began contemplating the next move to quit her day job and run the business as an affiliate supplier as she put plans to go solo. That is non-negotiable self-development next big step.

3. Don't Freak Out.

You have no prior knowledge what is around the corner in life. If you think of things going wrong, you freak out, and might never venture outside the house. You cannot succeed at work, in marriage, sports business, if you freak out. You can't undo mistakes from the past. But you can learn from past mistakes to avoid falling into the same pitfalls and repeat performance. Yesterday is gone. Tomorrow is yet to come. You only have today. Don't freak out. Make it count.

4. Listen to Your Inner Voice.

The process of individual inner awakening is laborious, sluggish and long depending on the urgency and magnitude of the task at hand. Resources you need for inner awakening are within reach all the time. Listening to your inner voice is first mentioned in chapter two in connection with staying focused to rise above the challenges of negative thoughts.

Listening to the inner voice initiatives evaluation and links individual potential to productivity. That is what Sandra did. That was the next move I made to change careers from sound engineering to online freelance writing. Read about my personal experience on the power of positive thinking for self-development in chapter six. It is your turn.

5. Banish Fear Out of Your Life

How much would you accomplish in life, if fear is not a major factor? You would do great exploits. There would be no anxiety over the future. Whatever your heart desires is within reach. But you are assailed by fear and doubt every day. Is there hope of overcoming fear? Yes there is. It's not easy to rise above the murky waters of fear in life, but it is possible.
Try out the simple exercise at the end of this chapter to help you face fear with courage.

Chapter 5 – Summary

Chapter five encourages you to be nice to yourself, to hang on to progress because you are ready for self-development. Follow these three things with five principles to make self-development dream a reality.

The five principles require you take the next big step, trust your instincts, don't freak out, and listen to your inner voice to banish fear out of your life. These five non-negotiable principles set self development foundation.

Exercise

You have a job interview coming up. This job opportunity has greater future prospects, if you can ace the interview. Here is what you need to do.

First, take seven deep breathes prior to the interview to relax your muscles. You have plenty of time to do this.

Second, visualize the outcome. Stay your mind on positive outcome. You have nothing to lose, and everything to gain.

Third, focus beyond the interview. Suspend all your prejudices for a moment to concentrate on this exercise. This exercise costs nothing but it could make the difference whether you get or lose this job opportunity. You are now good and ready to face the panel. That wasn't so hard was it?

Chapter 6 - How Self-Development Establish Success in Life.

You struggled for years to get your act together and live your dreams in life. If it's not finances putting your business out of joint, you increasingly worry over failing health and fitness. You fear the squabble in marriage relationship could cause you another stroke. You have changed careers more than thrice. You used to have strong personality, but not anymore. Is there an end to these challenges in life?

Any of these issues suggests you are not living the life you deserve. You know family and friends living their dreams. How do they do it? You have asked this question umpteenth time with little success for a suitable answer.

This chapter shows three simple ways to stop worrying and start living the life you deserve, by drawing on the best six self-development pieces of advice from life coaches to make the move for a change now in three simple steps.

Three Ways to Start Living the Life You Deserve

1. Rekindle Your Dream

When you are under 15, life is exciting. You turn twenty, and life is entertaining. By the time you cross the dividing line of youth and old age 40, life is endurance. No matter how old you are, you experience challenges in life. But despite the passing of time, your dreams stay intact.

Dreams form the foundation of your life. You wanted to grow up and become a doctor, business person, rich and famous. You are lucky if you have achieved all of your dreams in life. In most cases, what you wanted to become in youth isn't what you ended up doing for a living. Did the dream fizzle out and die with time? You used to talk about and share your dreams with friends and family members.

If you don't remember those dreams now, others do. Ask. Someone will be glad to refresh your memory. Your life has moved in a different direction. But there is no reason you cannot rekindle your dreams as a hobby, exercise, or side hustle.

2.   Vision and Mission Statements.

You don't have well written vision and mission statements similar to the ones of companies, organizations and businesses. But you do have a vision and mission to fulfill in life. Your vision and mission statements are not written on aboard or across the wall of a building for all to see.

Your vision and mission statements are in your heart. They cannot be erased or worn out by rigors of climate. Something is bound to trigger them. It could be tragedy. You might be reminded by a friend or family. The important thing is you alone can turn your dreams into reality.

Vision clarifies blurred image of the life you once dreamed about. Think of your vision in life as a dream written down on a piece of paper. Take that step and write your vision and mission down if you have not done so already.

3. Keep a Journal

Do you keep a journal? Most people don't. Keeping a journal is as easy as having to do list in a diary. A diary is a record of your daily life activities. The journal is a record of goals, and values. You also enter feelings, challenges and accomplishments in the journal. Evaluation and monitoring are two notable benefits of keeping a journal. Your journal goal entries have set dates. The journal shows whether you have achieved set goals or not. Here are six questions to get you started making journal entries.

What do you do for a living?
How much do you earn or expect to earn in 5, 7, 10 years?
Who are your friends?
How much quality time do you spend with family, friends and loved ones?

When do you break off from regular work?
How do you spend your free time?

This list is not exhaustive. Your life and experiences are different, so is your journal. Come up with a suitable list which addresses areas which need improvement in your life. This is your life. You are responsible how you want to live it. Change takes time. If you don't start self-development now, your life will be the same five ten years to come. Keep a journal to assist you evaluate and monitor your life every step of the way.

If you read all books and blog posts from life coaches on self-development, and listen to top motivational speakers, would your life change? It might or it might not. In most cases, it might not. That does not suggest the ideas contained in these books, blog posts and motivational speeches don't work. No one knows the score better than I do. My life was changed overnight from reading one self-development book.

Most of us picture unexpected life happenings in dark terms. I woke up on a strange bed in October 2004. The smell of medicine reminded me this was the hospital and not my house. It did not matter how long I was hospitalized, or that I had been in a coma for weeks. What freaked me out is the loss of hearing on both ears. All that was left of my once comfortable life was a huge black space spanning time and eternity. After five years of struggle to adjust and manage without hearing, Melanie, our first twin daughter handed me the first self-development book.

"Here dad, got you a book to read," Melanie announced, as she placed "Awaken the Giant Within," by Anthony Robbins on my hands. I wasn't aware, let alone heard books on the science of self-development exist at this point.

I couldn't put this book down for three reasons. One, Melanie borrowed it from her next door neighbor. Two, I should have left the previous day. Three, I needed something tangible to engage my creative mind.

Reading "Awaken the Giant Within," by Anthony Robbins transformed my life inside out overnight. This book opened my eyes of understanding. I learned many valuable lessons from reading this book plus 35+ others on self-development.

Three steps, situation analysis, sense of direction and setting achievable goals stood between my old and new life. These three in addition to five common lessons from reading different self-development books set my foot on self-development path. The lessons from these books worked for me. They will do the same for you provided your heart is in self-development.

Six Best Self-Development Pieces of Advice from Life Coaches.

1. Be Real

Self-motivation without action is worthless. You have met or know many pretenders in life. You might be one of them. Pretenders are normal ordinary human beings. Caroline, 30+ year old single woman is eager to start a serious relationship leading to marriage. But the moment a man pops the big question, she says,

"Give me time to think about it." Caroline is known among her girlfriends for pestering men to make commitment in relationships. Yet when the time comes, she is unprepared. You wonder why. Barbra has a different story to tell about relationship but the trend of thought is similar.

"What did you say?" Barbra asks as if she is short of hearing. You are unique and special. That is enough reason to be real.

2. Be Content in Life

You will never have enough of anything; let alone what you don't need. You think having a good car, buying a house outright, going on vacation abroad, having money stashed in the bank would make you happy. None of these items guarantees happiness.

You think life is better with salary increase, double profit margin in business, meeting and marrying someone special, setting aside money for retirement. These are legitimate human needs and desires, but they don't promise happiness. The more you acquire of this and that, the more you want. So what is the secret to happiness in life?

Be content with what you have. Spend time doing what you love and money will flow into your life in unexpected ways. Ask any life coach. You run the risk of stress, depression, heart attack or stroke if you have no peace of mind and heart.

3. Real Change is from Within

You can't change your spouse's mind. He/she is unique. He might keep you awake at night with snoring. He alone can change that habit. Change is linked to thoughts. Thoughts are exclusive to individuals. You only have control over your thoughts not his/hers.

Real change comes from within not without. If the guy wants to snoring, he will. You can't make him.

You will Laugh Again

Laughter is not only the best medicine; it's the only free medication with huge returns on investment. I did not laugh for a month. There was nothing to laugh about. I was in a comma for two weeks and the doctors made it clear to my family,

"This man will not live beyond ten days in this condition." I had forgotten how good laughing is Phoebe, our last born girl cracked me up three months later. I have since made the effort to laugh more. It is hard to laugh at nothing. You need to hear jokes. I am deaf, so nothing comes through that way to make me laugh. But I discovered different ways to make me laugh again.

Prank comedy show does it for me all the time. I can burst into eye watering laughter from watching video clips online. I don't need to hear what is said. "Action speaks louder than words," at least for me they do. You have a good pair of ears to tune into all frequencies with laughter lines. Are you laughing enough? What is stopping you from enjoying a good laugh? Laughter is good for your physical, psychological and spiritual wellness, and it is also free.

4. Imaginary Enemies.

"Imagination rules the world." Adolf Hitler is portrayed in literature as cruel and evil. You could come up with all kinds of negative adjectives to describe Hitler. What if you were tasked to find and write one or two good things about this man in exchange for pay?

You would get something special to say about the man Hitler. Think of Hitler as a man with larger than life imagination to rule the world. How many people have you met in life with this kind of imagination Hitler had? Now let's narrow this conversation down to you.

You are not proud of all the things you have done in life. If you had a second chance, and exposure to self-development, you would do better in different areas of your life. Imagination would be the driving force fueling your success steam. You have that second chance waiting around the corner to improve where you failed by shunning imaginary enemies.

Remember Maltz CRAFT acronym in chapter two. You can cancel negative thoughts, replace them with positive ones, affirm them in the theatre of your imagination with positive affirmations, and focus on the ultimate price as you train the mind to stay on positive mental attitude wavelength.

5. Do it Now

In today's rapidly changing world, an increasing number of businesses choose IT solutions to speed up productivity. You cannot afford to lag behind. Now is the right time. If you drag your feet in business, the opportunity is taken up by your competitor.

Putting off things derails self-development in all areas of life. You can't exercise only when it feels right. In your dreams you do. In real life, exercising forty minutes, thrice a week minimum will keep you from running to the doctor. Life is busy. The only time to get things done is now.

Make Self-Development Move to Change Now.

You have succeeded in the past. You can do it again.
…"Courage is not the absence of fear, it's the willingness to face it in spite of how you feel," Jeff Goins wrote in the book "The Art of Works." You can face today's challenges by using past success encounters as springboard, when you are ready for change, and aware something good is about to happen. The following three simple steps will guide your steps to change now.

1. Use Past Success to Encounter Present Challenge

You had a stomach full of butterflies, first time on a date. But you did ok. The time is right for another romantic relationship milestone. This is it. This is the big one you have been waiting for all your life. You finally met your soul mate. You asked the lady once to go out on a date with you and she did not object. You have been going steady. It feels right. You can see it in her eyes, and feel it in your bones. You are ready to make the move based on your past success.

2. Know When You are Ready for Change

I closed down the business office in 2007 despite being my only source of income. I couldn't cope with the stress of working hours. Finally, I had to close shop, go back home without future income prospect.

Looking back now, this decision tuned out as the best. Something good will come up, I thought. And indeed, online freelance writing was waiting; only I didn't know it at the time. All I knew is my heart's readiness to call it a day at the office. Positive thinking nudged me to take the next bold step.

You have the idea of setting up and running a small home based online business. The opportunity is here. You know you are ready. You have done the homework. You secured source of funds whether from personal savings or loan, to start the business while maintaining your day job. Do it now because something good is about to happen.

3. Something Good is About to Happen.

Whenever you are in a tight spot, call it between a stone and a hard rock, remember something good is about to happen. The tendency is fasten your eyes on the closed door. You miss to scan the horizon for open doors of opportunities. You are undecided, the situation is unpredictable.

Follow your heart. That is what I did to close down the office. Today, I run the house office. It's convenient, and less demanding. No rent. No need to dress up and it pays the bills. Did I know something good was about to happen? Not exactly, but positive thinking led me down that road.

Chapter 6 – Summary

Self-development is not rocket science. You can read and listen to brilliant ideas from life coaches. But it is up to you to use common sense to make the ideas work. In simple language, self-development is organized common sense.

Start living the life you deserve by taking into consideration the best six pieces of advice from life coaches to make self-development move in chapter six.

Chapter 7 - The Place of Positive Thinking Beyond Self-Development in Life

Chapter four briefly touched on happiness. Chapter seven, forecasts beyond self-development to examine expected happiness ultimate price. Most happy people have two common qualities in dealing with life's challenges. One, happy people are focused. Two happy people are not cynical. Let's examine each of these two qualities and illustrate them with practical life experience then proceed to emphasize the importance of lessons from life to assist you stick to your dreams.

Two Superior Qualities of Happy People.

1. Stay Focused.

You admire happy people. Life is fun if you are happy. The secret to happiness is out. A happy person is purpose driven. He/she has identified the one thing in life that makes him/her happy.

A happy person sets about how to get things done. Who wants to spend time sulking in life? Develop a thick skin with the power of positive thinking to enjoy real happiness in life. That is what makes life exciting and worth living. Psychologists' research studies reveal that happy people live better than average.

"The true secret of happiness lies in taking a genuine interest in all the details of daily life," William Morris said. Happy people are optimistic.

School curriculum does not offer a course on happiness. Life does. And most life lessons are free. But it takes effort to learn by following in the footsteps of a happy person.

Having something to look forward to sets your mind in motion to think and act as if the idea is a done deal. You breathe in and exhale what you want out of life. You are in control of your life. Keep at it. Stay focused in the field of preference and choice with positive thinking.

2. Stop Being Cynical.

Challenges in life are not meant to drown you in a sea of sorrow, but prompt you to take action. You get the opportunity to seek alternative suitable solutions to the challenging situation. Doctors told me,

"Be content deaf the rest of your life." I could have fallen into piece. But would that change the situation? No. I looked long and hard, searched my heart. I thought about what good could come out of this physical challenge then took steps to adjust and cope with deafness. I would still be drifting along with the crowd without a definite purpose if I wasn't deaf today.

Lessons from Life.

1. Learn Life's Lessons

You are upset whenever your comfort zone in life is disturbed. You can do one of two things, learn or run from reality. Talk to anyone who has been in a similar situation. You will discover that positive thinking gave the person reason to go on. That is how I started writing online.

You cannot miss something good even in a restricted world such as mine. In the process, you develop a thick skin to hang in there. That is positive thinking in action.   Maxwell Maltz CRAFT acronym ends with training.

Your brain thinks of one thing at a time. Try focusing on two or more issues at a time. The dominant thought has the upper hand. This is a huge advantage in training the mind. Focus on positive, and the mind will throw up positive thoughts. Negative thoughts have no foot hold. Think of the presence of positive and negative thoughts in terms of light and darkness.

Whenever light is introduced, darkness simply melts away. Light and darkness cannot co-exist. The same is true with negative and positive thoughts.

2. Stick to Your Dreams.

Picture an athlete practicing to make the team selection to represent his/her country at the Olympic Games. He/she spends time practicing. Practice is the one thing athletes do more besides regular normal life activities. An athlete is clear about what he/she wants to achieve. Clarity leads to contentment and contentment is demonstrated through happiness.
Positive affirmations and inspirational quotes are two of the best methods to use in developing positive mental attitude._You have many reasons to celebrate happiness. Life is a precious free gift to be thankful for.

Think of the opportunities life presents. Life is bright if that is what you are looking for and sad if negativity fills your heart. Be happy. It costs nothing but the gains are enormous.

Good or bad attitude is a choice you make. If you wake up in a foul carry forward mood from last night. Your mind shifts through the rubble of negative thoughts. The day is ruined before the show is on the road.

Picture this. You have a small disagreement with the spouse in the house. You fly off to go for drinks. You have taken one too many of the swallow but insist on driving yourself home in the wee hours of the night. You are courting trouble.

You know better than to drive under the influence of alcohol. You were better off staying calm to let tempers cool down at home than tear off to the bar. You soon discover the disagreement isn't worth the sweat. Tearing away in a fit of rage is not the solution. You can work yourself out of a bad situation through positive thinking. Here are three benefits of positive thinking on the go.

3. Positive thinking leaves no room for negative thoughts to settle in the mind.

4. You can raise your standard of living with positive thinking. Your brain and body will corporate to give you the desired outcome.

5. You develop self-confidence through positive thinking than you would with negative thoughts.

Your life is in your hands to do as you please. Choose positive over negative thoughts and life becomes one big adventure.

Overall Summary

Chapter six is your clarion call to action to start living the life you deserve now. You have come a long way from discovering you create your thoughts in chapter one featuring body and brain connectivity and the significance of positive thinking in self-development. There is no turning back on self-development.

You know thoughts shape your personality from seven ways to adjust and manage your thoughts in chapter two.

You took four steps to overcome negative thoughts in chapter three to realize real life transformation.

You could not wait to unleash the power of positive thinking through self-development with seven ways to renew the brain by improving the body to stimulate the brain with six must do things in chapter four.

Once you set up self-development foundation with three simple actions in chapter five, you are able to take five steps to maintain positive mental attitude.

In chapter six you start to live the life you deserve by heeding the best six pieces of advice from life coaches to establish self-development.

What is the next big thing? Life continues, and so does positive thinking beyond self-development in chapter seven. You are good and ready to live the life you want.